CW00889538

THE QU
SPIRITUAL HUNGER

THE QUEST FOR
SPIRITUAL HUNGER

by
Roberts Liardon

ALBURY PUBLISHING

10th Printing
Over 65,000 in Print

The Quest For Spiritual Hunger
ISBN 1-88008-977-7

Copyright © 1987 by Roberts Liardon Ministries
P.O. Box 30710
Laguna Hills, California 92654

Published by ALBURY PUBLISHING
P.O. Box 470406
Tulsa, Oklahoma 74137

CONTENTS

1
DEVELOPING A SPIRITUAL HUNGER

Blessed are they which do hunger and thirst after righteousness: for they shall be filled.

Matthew 5:6

At the tender age of 12, Jesus hungered for the things of the Spirit of God. The wisdom in Jesus at this age baffled the godly leaders of Jerusalem. His spiritual wisdom also baffled His parents!

After being in Jerusalem for the Passover Feast, Jesus did not join the group returning to Galilee because of His great interest in the affairs of His heavenly Father, His hunger for spiritual things.

Every year his parents went to Jerusalem for the Feast of the Passover. When he was twelve years old, they went up to the Feast, according to the custom. After the Feast was over, while his parents were returning home, *the boy Jesus stayed behind in Jerusalem, but they were unaware of it*. Thinking he was in their company, they traveled on for a day. Then they began looking for him among their relatives and friends. When they did not find him, they went back to Jerusalem to look for him. After three days they found him in the temple courts, sitting among the teachers, listening to them and asking them questions. Everyone who heard him was amazed at his understanding and his answers. When his parents saw him, they were astonished. His mother said to him, *"Son, why have you treated us like this? Your father and I have been anxiously searching for you."*

"Why were you searching for me?" he asked. **"Didn't you know I had to be in my Father's house?"** **But they did not understand what he was saying to them.**

Then he went down to Nazareth with them and was obedient to them. But his mother treasured all these things in her heart. And Jesus grew in wisdom and stature, and in favor with God and men.

Luke 2:41-52 NIV

At 12 years of age, Jesus was about kingdom business. The most important business you can attend to is your Father's business, no matter what your age. This is the hour when children (some even younger than 12) will step forth into kingdom business as leaders!

When I first started walking with God, everybody told me the things I *could not* do. No one told me the things I *could* do. But there was such a hunger on the inside of me! I still have that hunger for the things of God, and I wanted God big — not small. I was taught as a child that *God is big, and you have to pay a price to get Him.*

Salvation is a free gift, but there is more than being born again and going to Heaven. You must pay a price to get that "something more."

I remember sometimes I would say to my mother or my grandmother, "I don't want to read the Bible. I think it's boring. I don't want to pray anymore. I think that's boring, too."

They would respond, "That's what you think!"

Then they would get after me.

Grandma trained me. A lot of people do not have grandparents or parents to train them as I did.

Grandma was persistent in training me. She helped develop a spiritual hunger in me.

If there were more teachers like my grandmother, we would live in a better world. We would live in the realm of the Spirit continually, the realm where Christians are supposed to live.

The reason the glory of God rarely comes, or the reason people are not flowing with the Holy Spirit, is because they do not hunger for the things of God.

A mental desire to see the spectacular is not spiritual hunger but a soulish desire. A mental desire will not get you to the place where you will be led by the Holy Spirit, nor will it help you flow with the Holy Spirit.

You must make yourself "eat" righteousness until your appetite desires more righteousness. Grandma made me "eat" righteousness. She made me "eat" John 3:16. She made me read my Bible from cover to cover every year that she had charge of me.

I did not realize the forces of evil that Grandma kept off me until she finally turned me loose. Once she released me from her protective authority, those forces hit me hard.

I thought, *Dear God, Grandma. Let me get back under your control. It's easier there.*

She said, "No. Now you must grow up and be a man."

Grandma had wisdom regarding spiritual training. Now that I am older, I have not departed from the way of righteousness, because Grandma trained me to hunger and thirst after righteousness, not after the things of the world. The desire for righteousness got into my blood. Now I desire the things of the Spirit.

Developing an Appetite
For Things of the Spirit

To develop a spiritual hunger in me, Grandma made me devour the Scriptures. If I was not reading the Word, I was hearing the Word. She played cassette tapes of spiritual teaching and preaching continually. The Word of God prevailed in our home to the point where there was nothing else to see or hear but the things of righteousness.

We fellowshiped with people who possessed spiritual hunger. We were not allowed to associate with people who did not desire the things of God.

Television was monitored. Music was monitored. Our home was like a military academy in some ways; however, divine love flowed freely, causing everything to function properly. If you do not have love in the home, you will have problems. Love has the same effect as oil in an engine.

Many people try to do what Grandma did, but they use the power of the rod without the oil of love. You will experience problems with teenagers, whether there is discipline or lack of discipline, *if* there is no real love and caring involved.

The reason some teenagers rebel at the things of God when they are made to read the Bible or attend church is because there is discipline and not enough love in their home. Those parents need to ask God for a greater dimension of His love.

Done in love, the rod means correction. Otherwise, spanking is punishment. All of the Bible verses dealing with bringing up children mean correction or instruction in the original languages — not punishment.

The natural man has a built-in desire for truth and reality. We are created that way. Most of the time, however, we are "programmed" by the world's thinking and the world system into accepting a counterfeit, so that the world's "truth and reality" is really falsehood and unreality.

Because of Grandma's correction and instruction, I enjoyed the Bible by the time she placed me on my own. I enjoyed hearing about the deep things of God. I hungered for the things of the Spirit.

Many parents are saying, "What is wrong with our children? We've trained them, so what is wrong?"

You cannot say you have trained your children if you have been setting a wrong example in front of them. You cannot just *tell* children what to do. *You must show them by example.*

I am trying to encourage the Body of Christ to wake up and walk in God's truth, so we can go on home to Heaven where we belong. However, so many people are playing games with God, not hungering or thirsting for His righteousness.

I saw people in Africa who died because they were physically hungry.

Even those Africans who were not starving had a hunger for sweets, because they have little of that sort of food. We took candy into Mozambique to give to the children. Some of them had never seen a piece of candy, but once they heard about it or tasted it, they developed a hunger for it. They wanted it!

The man who took us into the little village in Mozambique said, "Be careful with that candy, because the children will jump you for it."

I pulled the bag of candy out of my pocket and said, "You want a piece?"

There were only three pieces of candy in my hand, but they knew I had more. Just think! An American missionary holding his hand up, asking:

"You want a piece of candy?"

The children could not understand a word I said, but one of the people with me yelled, "Roberts, be careful!"

I thought, *What can these little kids do to me?*

Holding my hand down to the children, I looked at the candy to see how fast it would go — but I did not know my fingers would go with it!

They began hitting my hand and pulling on my fingers for more. Those children hungered after that candy! They wanted it!

I began to pray, "Lord, help me get loose from these children."

Finally, I managed to get back in the truck, get the door closed, and get someone to join me on the other side of the seat.

I said, "Here is the bag of candy. Count to three, grab as much as you can, and throw it out the door. That way, we'll be safe."

My point is this: *If you do not hunger after the things of God as those children hungered for candy, when things of God come to you, you will not recognize them.*

Many people do not have any hunger at all for the things of God.

Why are people missing the moves of God that are happening in their midst right now? They are not hungering and thirsting after the things of God.

The African children hungered after that candy. They are waiting for the next foreign visitor to come through so they can attack him for another bag of candy.

That is how we need to be with the things of God — enjoying what we now have but constantly hungering for more. We need to want *more* of God, to want His presence, to want to walk in His glory, to want His power, to want to talk with Him as a friend. We need to want more of Him!

You have to walk the floor as I did when Grandma said, "Now, it's up to you."

She was firm and determined with me, so the only thing I knew to do was what she did — press on in for more of the things of God.

I would walk the floor, saying, "I want more of You, God. Holy Spirit, flow through me. Holy Spirit, lead me. Teach me. Guide me. I want more of You. I want all I can get, then I want some more."

How long do you have to walk the floor and say that until you start desiring the things of God? Sometimes it takes months.

Make your mind imagine the things of God. Make your mouth declare your hunger for God. I made myself do this. I did not want to at first, but I did it anyway. Now, I have more of God. I have Him all over me, in me, out of me, and around me.

I spoke these things until I developed a hunger for God. He will answer you when He sees that you have a true hunger for Him. As I walked the floor, I was developing my inner man (my spirit).

By the Holy Spirit in my spirit, I began calling those things which were not as though they were. I received more of God. The gifts of the Holy Spirit began to flow through me. I began to see visions. My spiritual hunger increased continually, and I still want more of God.

God Only Answers One Hunger

When I was in Africa, I wanted an American hamburger so badly I could almost *see* a McDonald's. I ate African food, but I was hungry for a hamburger. When I arrived back in the United States at Tulsa International Airport, I did not say, "Hello," or "It's good to see you."

I said, "Where's a McDonald's? I want a hamburger. I want it *now!*"

A specific hunger had developed in me that nothing else satisfied. I got a McDonald's hamburger, devoured it, and went back for another.

There are all kinds of hunger, but there is only one hunger that God answers, according to the Gospel of Matthew.

Blessed are they which do hunger and thirst after righteousness: for they shall be filled.

Matthew 5:6

How long do you have to hunger like this before God answers you? Until there is a proven hunger.

Some folks satisfy their hunger with the false. Other people give up too easily. I could have given up my hunger for a hamburger while I traveled through

14

Africa, but I kept it. I knew that hamburger was out there somewhere. I got to the point where I was willing to take a morning flight, eat a hamburger, and fly back! *I wanted a hamburger.* Do you understand that kind of hunger? I would probably have given $100 for a $.39 hamburger. I mean, I *wanted* one.

To be spiritually filled and to have spiritual growth, you must hunger after the things of God. Grandma developed that kind of hunger in me. After I was on my own, I continued to develop that hunger. I became starved for more of God.

Spiritual Hunger Can Be Satisfied But Never Vanquished

After you attain your goal, spiritual hunger always reaches for more. For several months, I have imagined what the things of God will be like in the next move of His Spirit. What will happen to people when the glory hits? How will I react? The glory is just now beginning to hit a little here and there. Yet even now, people are being turned away from meetings because there is no room. Ministries are beginning to explode with growth.

My ministry is beginning to explode because at 9 and 10 years of age I was saying, "I want more of God. I hunger after God. I am thirsty for God's living water. I am thirsty for God's knowledge. I am hungry."

The Bible promises that you shall be filled, yet the hunger for God never comes to an end but goes on forever. To go to the next realm of glory, you must be filled with the one you are on.

Many people get saved and baptized in the Holy Spirit, believe in healing, know the Word works, and they are happy — but they stay on the same level of glory, which results in a spiritual bloating, not spiritual growth. They do not look for a new realm of glory; they are content where they are.

While you are feasting in one realm of glory, your eyes should look for the *next* realm of glory. That is the way we need to be to flow with the Spirit of God.

True spiritual hunger will cause you to devour the Word of God and go back for more. Spiritual hunger recognizes spiritual food. You will recognize the genuine, and you will recognize the counterfeit. Spiritual hunger will cause the things of the natural realm to become less significant in your life.

The Russians know that if the people are starved, they will be easy to rule. Once they bring food, the starving people will do anything the authorities say and think whatever the rulers want them to think. A starving people can be the most militant, mean, and successful force on the earth.

If we are desirous of the things of God, we must be very militant in getting them. That means we will break down the doors of darkness to get the true light.

Truly Hungry People Are Violent People

Starving people are violent people. If you are not "violent" where spiritual food is concerned, you are not truly hungry.

If I said to some people, "I hunger for the things of God," they would think I was weird.

But you have to be like that. I believe this kind of spiritual hunger was what Jesus had in mind when he said:

And from the days of John the Baptist until now the kingdom of heaven suffereth violence, *and the violent take it by force.*

Matthew 11:12

Teenagers, listen to me: You need to walk the floor, confess the Word, and meditate the Word. Even if it seems strange, meditate on God and on the things of God. Let your spirit put visions in your mind.

I have meditated on the outreaches of Roberts Liardon Ministries for years. I have meditated on missionary work for years. I have meditated on my traveling ministry for years. I would see myself enlarging my circles all the time. I would see myself overseas preaching to the masses. I would see myself building up the people. I have dreamed and dreamed and dreamed until today these things are beginning to happen. Yet I am still hungering for more.

Deep calleth unto deep . . . (Ps. 42:7).

If there is a deep *calling,* there must be a deep to *answer* the call. If there is a hunger, there must be something to satisfy that hunger. If you are hungering for more power, there must be power to receive. If you are hungering for more love, there must be more love to receive.

The late evangelist William Branham told the story of a little boy who ate things containing sulphur. Once, he ate his bicycle pedal. That sounds extreme! They took him to the doctor, who found that the little boy's body craved sulphur so much that he ate things

17

containing it without knowing why or even knowing those things contained sulphur.

I have seen African pastors hunger for the things of God in a similar manner, and some of them have only one or two pages of the Bible. Yet they are doing the right things, not knowing they are following principles of the Word of God. As a result, they are getting blessed.

That is the way all Christians are supposed to be. We are to hunger after the things of God and not to search or hunger after anything or anyone *but* God.

The Bible says that if you hunger after God, you will be filled. If you hunger after *spiritual* things, God will make sure you have everything you need in the *natural*.

God satisfies my every desire. I am happy with the clothes I wear, the money He provides, the traveling I do. I am happy with the ministry God has given me. I believe the reason God satisfies my every need is because I hunger after Him more every day.

Spiritual Hunger Brings Blessings

If you want to be blessed in the natural realm, get your eyes on God. Get your hunger off cars or bank accounts and get it on God. Now I am not looking for a large personal bank account. However, if it comes, I am not going to be dumb enough to turn it down.

Some people think that being spiritual means rejecting every material blessing and suffering. But God says He will cause the wealth of the wicked to come into our hands.

A good man leaveth an inheritance to his children's children: *and the wealth of the sinner is laid up for the just.*

Proverbs 13:22

When wealth comes, I am certainly not going to return it! I will receive it in Jesus' Name.

As I walk and hunger after the things of God, He gives me everything that I need. I am trying to carry you to a new level of spiritual hunger. Look for God in everything!

2

MATURATION IN THE SCHOOL OF THE HOLY SPIRIT

Regardless of your natural age, once you have developed a spiritual hunger, paid a visit to the Father's house, and received His direction for your life, there is a time of preparation that must take place before you step into your call.

I have seen people ignore the need for preparation time or abort this special time only to end up on the spiritual trash heap, no good to anyone — all because they were not spiritually ready for their particular assignment. God's timing is as important as His call.

It is not God's intent that anyone end up defeated because of not knowing how to daily make war with the evil elements of the world. I have seen this type of defeat overtake far too many of God's chosen, called, anointed, and commissioned vessels.

Whether you are called to preach, teach, or simply to run a Christian bookstore, there is a need for both natural and spiritual preparation. However, natural preparation without adequate spiritual preparation will not work. Spiritual preparation cannot be shirked. Little or no preparation sets the stage for a difficult time in undertaking any assignment from on high. You will get beaten up in some realm, if your spiritual preparation is not adequate. You will end up doing nothing for God.

I have seen people go off to Bible school, and when they complete this short time of preparation and training, they think they are ready to conquer the entire world! After this natural preparation in knowledge of the Word, they need the spiritual preparation in the School of the Holy Spirit, which is attained only on your knees in prayer.

There is more to preparation than going to Bible school. I do not want to see more young, anointed ministers of the Gospel devastated beyond repair and losing the harvest of souls they were to gather, because of being ill-prepared spiritually.

Learn Spiritual Things Early

My grandmother is an old-time Pentecostal who, as a teenager, attended an Akron, Ohio, church where "hellfire and brimstone" was preached. Her church taught that you would not go to Heaven unless you were baptized in the Holy Spirit! (Thank the Lord, we have come a long way since that time.) Grandma met people in her church who had been a part of the Azusa Street revival — the beginning of modern-day Pentecostalism.

The pastor of this church began a 24-hour prayer chain, and Grandma volunteered to pray an hour a day as part of this chain. People in her day seemed to be more committed than believers are today. It is difficult to get people to pray three seconds for a church or for anything else.

Eternal things are far more important than natural things. We need to spend more time developing the things of the Spirit in our lives.

Grandma's father taught her, "Never tell a lie. Once you have given your word, stick to it at any cost."

That is a good philosophy for anyone! We need that preached more often from church pulpits. Once you say you will do something, be willing to die to keep your word. Your word is your bond, not something you just let float around with no meaning or commitment attached.

Grandma gave her word that she would pray an hour a day as part of the Rev. McKinney's prayer chain. She told me she would set her clock for an hour, but after praying for everything she could think of, found she had only prayed 10 minutes. Prayer is a discipline. Just like exercise, you become better with practice.

Grandma said, ''I would not give up, because I had committed myself to that hour. I told that man of God that I would pray an hour for his church, so I was going to do it or die.''

And she thought she *was* going to die. She would pray about everything she knew to pray about, which back then, included only her neighbors, the mayor, policemen, prostitutes, and unsaved loved ones. That was about it. She was involved in her own little world. However, Grandma hungered and thirsted for the things of God, and it was during this time that she developed into a mighty prayer warrior. She got to the point that the minute she hit her knees, the Holy Spirit came on the scene. There are few people I know like that.

Teaching by Example

Grandma always enforced what Jesus said. I will never forget the day she looked at me and said, ''*If you are ever going to be a successful businessman, or a minister of the Gospel, you must know how to pray. So let's begin right now.''*

She did not even *ask* me if I wanted to pray. She *made* me pray. She dragged me into a prayer life. The first day, I did not want to pray. I wanted to watch television. Thank God that Grandma was persistent.

She said, ''Get on your knees.'' I obeyed. I was very young at the time.

''Throw your hands up and praise God,'' she told me.

I did.

She said, ''Repeat after me,'' led me in my first Holy Spirit prayer, and never said amen. She just started in praying on her own.

Kneeling down beside me, she would say, ''I don't want you to move from this spot. If you do, when I get through praying, you are going to get it!

Grandma would pray for hours. She meant business when she prayed.

She would pray, ''God help our churches to honor the Bible. Fill the preachers with Holy Spirit fire. If they do not honor you, remove them from the pulpits. Get Holy Spirit men in the pulpits, not dead ones.''

We need that kind of praying today. Grandma knew that dead preachers produce dead people. Fiery preachers produce fire in the church — fire for God and fire for the things of God. Hallelujah! I have seen Grandma literally ''pray in'' revivals.

When Grandma came against the forces of darkness in prayer, that is when things would get interesting. When she started fighting demons, that is when I became interested.

My sister and I watched her. I learned a lot by watching her, and your children will learn best by your example. They will learn best by seeing *you* pray, by seeing *you* fight the forces of darkness, by seeing *you* intercede.

I thought everybody prayed like Grandma. I really did. It was a shock when I found out that few Christians prayed at all. I wondered what was wrong with everyone else's grandmothers. I wondered what was wrong with their homes. I was trained in spiritual things in my home. I received training alongside my grandmother and my mother.

I was not told, "Go to your room, pray, and read the Scripture by yourself."

Grandma showed me how to pray. She took me with her into the realm of the Spirit. She showed me how to fight demonic forces, how to get the bills paid, how to pray the right people into positions of leadership and the wrong ones out.

You can best show others how to be led by the Spirit of God through the life you live, not by what you say. Talk is cheap, especially in children's eyes. If you are not living what you say you believe, children will not buy what you say.

Grandma always told me, "Don't ever be ashamed of the Gospel. Don't ever be ashamed to yield to the Holy Spirit wherever you are."

I saw her walk down the aisles in the grocery store praying in tongues. That was normal for me. One night, God spoke to me in a grocery store and told me to cast the devil out of someone. I flinched a little, but I obeyed. I had learned it is best to obey!

When children are trained right, they will not depart from the ways of the Lord they they get old. If you want Holy Spirit-trained children, open your eyes and ears to what the Spirit of God is saying.

I am really tired of seeing my generation all goofed up. In most cases, it is the fault of parents who did not train their children in the ways of God while they were young.

Unity and Corporate Prayer

If any member of Grandma's family faces a situation where he or she cannot seem to pray through to victory, another family member is called, and they pray in agreement until the battle is won. When one family member hurts, we all hurt until we pray the situation through to victory.

We have agreed together in prayer until everyone's bills were paid. We have stood together until we saw many answers to prayer manifested. We have hounded Heaven's doors until God answered.

I believe sometimes God must have said, ''Let's answer their prayers so they will be quiet!''

We knew how to be persistent in prayer, which is one of the keys to a successful prayer life. Confession is important but must be reinforced with prayer to be effective.

I am convinced that corporate prayer, unity, and love are God's design for the entire Body of Christ.

Only in this manner will some of the hurdles we face be overcome in this day and hour. God is calling men and women to use power and discernment, sharpened through prayer. Then, everywhere we walk, we will tear the devil up.

The Book of Jude says:

> **But ye, beloved, building up yourselves on your most holy faith, praying in the Holy Ghost,**
>
> **Keep yourselves in the love of God, looking for the mercy of our Lord Jesus Christ unto eternal life.**
>
> Jude 21,22

I believe Grandma knew these verses very well, because when we came home from school, she would take us in a room, shut the door, and then say:

"Now, hit your knees. I want to hear you pray in tongues loud enough for both your ears and mine to hear."

Why did she do that? Because that attitude was the thing that strengthened us in boldness in the Lord, although it seemed weird at first.

If we did not pray loud enough, she would say, "I can't hear you!"

That is how to train your children in the ways of the Lord. That is how to teach them about the realm of the Spirit. That is how to teach them to discern a demon from an angel. That is where your children learn to know the voice of God from a human or demonic voice.

Grandma knew how to raise children, and she knew how to build churches. She would head up prayer groups and teach them exactly as she taught me. She would set the example of how to pray, and she would correct in love when someone got in the flesh. The results were that through the power of the Holy Spirit, both the individuals and the church were cleaned up.

Spiritual Training Must Begin in the Home

I am convinced that the training program that Grandma put me through is God-ordained for parents, not for Sunday School teachers, nursery school teachers, or Christian School teachers. The training of a child's spirit must begin *in the home*.

My early life consisted mostly of Grandma, God, me, and my bedroom. That is where I learned to pray. The day came when Grandma no longer had to push me into spiritual things, particularly in prayer. I had learned to enjoy praying with great boldness. I *desired* to pray in the Spirit. Everything else became secondary to me. I *hungered* for the things of the Spirit.

The day came when I would say, "Grandma, let's go pray."

She would answer, "We haven't had breakfast yet!"

I would respond, "I don't care. Let's pray, Grandma. Let's go set people free from devils! Let's pray for the man next door."

I would pray as long as I could and get as close to Grandma as I could, because the closer I was to her, the more I would be in the midst of the power of God when it fell. I wanted Grandma to get into that realm. I wanted the glory of God to hit. I enjoyed shaking under the power of God. I knew I would be strengthened when the glory hit.

When we prayed, I would make sure that Grandma was comfortable. I would make sure that she had her glass of water, her handkerchief, and her pillows. I would make sure the phone was off the hook. I would make sure no one came to the door. I knew prayer time was a time when we did not want to be disturbed in any way. No interruptions were allowed. That was the standard Grandma set.

When she prayed, I knew what every little grunt meant, and I would go get what she wanted. That is the way ministries need to treat the prophets of God today. A sigh from Grandma, and I knew what she wanted. A move of her little finger, and I knew what that meant. I knew Grandma better than anyone else knew her. That is the way you should be when a man or woman of God comes across your pathway. By the Spirit of God, you will know what is needed and what to say.

Grandma would discern through the Holy Spirit when family members were having difficulties, even those who lived at a great distance. She would just know it in the Spirit. She would pray, and I saw the manifestation to her prayers. Family members in difficulty soon were restored to God. Grandma had a "hotline" to God. I knew it because of the fruit of her labor. The Word of God says:

> **The eyes of the Lord are upon the righteous, and his ears are open unto their cry.**
>
> **The face of the Lord is against them that do evil, to cut off the remembrance of them from the earth.**
>
> **The righteous cry, and the Lord heareth, and delivereth them out of all their troubles.**
>
> Psalm 34:15-17

To survive in this hour, we must be keenly tuned to the Spirit of God. My human spirit was sharpened to hear the Spirit of God as I became Grandma's "Elisha." You need to train your children to be your "Elishas." Elisha knew everything about Elijah.

29

When it was time for Elijah to go home to Heaven, he asked Elisha, "What do you want of me? You have been a great blessing to me. You have helped me fight the battles. You have helped me run the race well. Now, what can I do for you?"

And it came to pass, when the Lord would take up Elijah into heaven by a whirlwind, that Elijah went with Elisha from Gilgal.

And Elijah said unto Elisha, Tarry here, I pray thee; for the Lord hath sent me to Bethel. And Elisha said unto him, As the Lord liveth, and as thy soul liveth, I will not leave thee. So they went down to Bethel.

And the sons of the prophets that were at Bethel came forth to Elisha, and said unto him, Knowest thou that the Lord will take away thy master from thy head to day? And he said, Yea, I know it; hold ye your peace.

And Elijah said unto him, Elisha, tarry here, I pray thee; for the Lord hath sent me to Jericho. And he said, As the Lord liveth, and as thy soul liveth, I will not leave thee. So they came to Jericho.

And the sons of the prophets that were at Jericho came to Elisha, and said unto him, Knowest thou that the Lord will take away thy master from thy head to day? And he answered, Yea, I know it; hold ye your peace.

And Elijah said unto him, Tarry, I pray thee, here; for the Lord hath sent me to Jordan. And he said, As the Lord liveth, and as thy soul liveth, I will not leave thee. And they two went on.

And fifty men of the sons of the prophets went, and stood to view afar off: and they two stood by Jordan.

And Elijah took his mantle, and wrapped it together, and smote the waters, and they were divided hither and thither, so that they two went over on dry ground.

And it came to pass, when they were gone over, that Elijah said unto Elisha, Ask what I shall do for thee, before I be taken away from thee. And Elisha said, I pray thee, let a double portion of thy spirit be upon me.

And he said, Thou hast asked a hard thing: nevertheless, if thou see me when I am taken from thee, it shall be so unto thee; but if not, it shall not be so.

And it came to pass, as they still went on, and talked, that, behold, there appeared a chariot of fire, and horses of fire, and parted them both asunder; and Elijah went up by a whirlwind into heaven.

And Elisha saw it, and he cried, My father, my father, the chariot of Israel, and the horsemen thereof. And he saw him no more: and he took hold of his own clothes, and rent them in two pieces.

He took up also the mantle of Elijah that fell from him, and went back, and stood by the bank of Jordan;

And he took the mantle of Elijah that fell from him, and smote the waters, and said, Where is the Lord God of Elijah? and when he also had smitten the waters, they parted hither and thither: and Elisha went over.

And when the sons of the prophets which were to view at Jericho saw him, they said, *The spirit of Elijah doth rest on Elisha.*

2 Kings 2:1-15a

3
SIN SQUELCHES
SPIRITUAL HUNGER

God wants a glorious Church — one without spot, wrinkle, or blemish. The spots, wrinkles, and blemishes are the sins of the believers, not the sins of unbelievers.

Sin is a killer! It will squelch spiritual hunger and block the flow of the Holy Spirit in your life. In fact, it will stop all the movement of the Spirit in your life.

In studying the lives of great preachers of the past, I have noticed that many of them lost their power, crowds, families, and even their own lives because of sin. They ended up losing everything.

We need to understand that there is no *degree* of sin in God's eyes. In today's society, we tend to place "degrees" on sins, thinking, *This one isn't too bad, but this other one is simply horrible.*

> Blessed is the man that walketh not in the counsel of the ungodly, nor standeth in the way of sinners, nor sitteth in the seat of the scornful.
>
> But his delight is in the law of the Lord; and in his law doth he meditate day and night.
>
> And he shall be like a tree planted by the rivers of water, that bringeth forth his fruit in his season; his leaf also shall not wither; and whatsoever he doeth shall prosper.
>
> Psalm 1:1-3

The Desire to Live a Holy Life

God's Word has a lot to say about living a holy and righteous life. If you truly hunger after the things of the Spirit of God, you will *desire* to live a holy life. Psalm 112:1-3 says:

> Praise ye the Lord. Blessed is the man that feareth the Lord, that delighteth greatly in his commandments.
>
> His seed shall be mighty upon earth: the generation of the upright shall be blessed.
>
> Wealth and riches shall be in his house: and his righteousness endureth for ever.

Psalm 119:1,2 says:

> Blessed are the undefiled in the way, who walk in the law of the Lord.
>
> Blessed are they that keep his testimonies, and that seek him with the whole heart.

It is God's desire that we be "perfect" in Him.

> Thou shalt be perfect with the Lord thy God.

Deuteronomy 18:13

God speaks to us again in Matthew 5:16 about letting the light of Christ radiate through us:

> Let your light so shine before men, that they may see your good works, and glorify your Father which is in heaven.

God spoke through Isaiah the prophet:

> And they shall call them, *The holy people,* The redeemed of the Lord: and thou shalt be called, Sought out, A city not forsaken.

Isaiah 62:12

The Kingdom of Heaven is prepared for the holy:

> Know ye not that the unrighteous shall not inherit the kingdom of God? Be not deceived: neither

34

fornicators, nor idolators, nor adulterers, nor effeminate, nor abusers of themselves with mankind,

Nor thieves, nor covetous, nor drunkards, nor revilers, nor extortioners, shall inherit the kingdom of God.

And such were some of you: but ye are washed, but ye are sanctified, but ye are justified in the name of the Lord Jesus, and by the Spirit of our God.

1 Corinthians 6:9-11

First Corinthians 6:17-20 says:

But he that is joined unto the Lord is one spirit.

Flee fornication. Every sin that a man doeth is without the body; but he that committeth fornication sinneth against his own body.

What? know ye not that your body is the temple of the Holy Ghost which is in you, which ye have of God, and ye are not your own?

For ye are bought with a price: therefore glorify God in your body, and in your spirit, which are God's.

God spoke through Paul saying, **Awake to righteousness.** That is a command, not an option!

Awake to righteousness, and sin not; for some have not the knowledge of God: I speak this to your shame.

1 Corinthians 15:34

Paul continued to write on the theme of holy living in his letter to the church at Galatia.

Be not deceived; God is not mocked: for whatsoever a man soweth, that shall he also reap.

For he that soweth to his flesh shall of the flesh reap corruption; and he that soweth to the Spirit shall of the Spirit reap life everlasting.

And let us not be weary in well doing: for in due season we shall reap, if we faint not.

Galatians 6:7-9

In essence, Paul was saying, "We are not called to filth; we are called to holiness."

For God hath not called us unto uncleanness, but unto *holiness*.

1 Thessalonians 4:7

The theme of *holiness* is also discussed by the apostle Peter:

But as he which hath called you is holy, so be ye holy in all manner of conversation;

Because it is written, Be ye holy; for I am holy.

1 Peter 1:15,16

Most believers have their outward men well-organized to avoid sin. However, internal "mental" sins will kill them if those sins are not dealt with.

***Let not* sin therefore reign in your mortal body, that ye should obey it in the lusts thereof.**

Neither yield ye your members as instruments of unrighteousness unto sin: but yield yourselves unto God, as those that are alive from the dead, and your members as instruments of righteousness unto God.

For sin shall not have dominion over you: for ye are not under the law, but under grace.

What then? shall we sin, because we are not under the law, but under grace? God forbid.

Know ye not, that to whom ye yield yourselves servants to obey, his servants ye are to whom ye obey; whether of sin unto death, or of obedience unto righteousness?

Romans 6:12-16

In verse 12, **let not** indicates that it is the believer's decision to sin or not to sin. **Let not** has everything to do with your personal will. *You* are the one who makes the decision to sin.

The Decision to Sin Begins in the Mind

The only thing the devil can do is offer you the temptation to sin. He puts the sin before you. However, *you* are the one who makes the decision, "Am I going to yield to sin or to God?"

Jesus speaks about "mental sins" in Matthew 5:

> **Ye have heard that it was said by them of old time, Thou shalt not commit adultery:**
>
> **But I say unto you, That whosoever looketh on a woman to lust after her hath committed adultery with her already in his heart.**
>
> Matthew 5:27,28

The mind must be renewed and transformed by the washing of the Word of God. Only then will you be rid of sinful thoughts and imaginations. A wandering mind may think on evil thoughts, such as adultery, but as believers, we are to think on those things which are true, honest, pure, lovely, and of good report. (Phil. 4:8.)

Sin will cause you to lose God's power, and sin will block your communication line to the Throne Room of God. God's glory and sin simply will *not* mix. They will *never* mix! Shake yourself free from sin completely so that you are prepared to taste of God's glory and live. If sin is not dealt with, when God's glory is released an explosion will take place resulting in judgment, even death at times.

Old-time preacher Jonathan Edwards preached a famous sermon entitled, "Sinners in the Hands of an Angry God." When he would preach this sermon, people would quake and shake in the middle of the service. But, contrary to popular opinion, this sermon was not about the wrath of God, but about His mercy.

Edwards was preaching about how forbearing God was when our unrighteousness comes into contact with His holiness, about what God has a perfect right to do — but doesn't because He loves us. We need some of that fear of God in our churches today.

You cannot go out and *knowingly* commit sin with the intention of asking for forgiveness the next morning. No, you cannot! It is just as easy to do right as it is to sin. In fact, it is easier. But *you* must make the decision whether to travel the road of sin or the road of righteousness.

Until you make the decision to live a life of holiness, your travels with God will be nonexistent. You see, there are no "big" or "little" sins with God. In His eyes, sin is sin.

When you willfully sin, you sow seed that will grow. The devil will make sure it is watered. That sin will bring forth the same kind of fruit. You sowed it, and you will reap the fruit thereof. God does not cause that seed to grow and produce. *You do.* To develop good fruit, you must see that it is watered with the Word.

What about the sin of ignorance? I used to preach a heavy-duty sermon, "Sin No More," in which I would provide people with an escape route. Everybody loved it!

I would say, "If you are ignorant, you can plead ignorance before the Throne of God, and He will okay it."

Then God showed me I was wrong.

The Spirit of God said to me, "When Jesus went to Heaven, He sent the Holy Spirit back to the earth — the Great Teacher — to guide us into *all truth.*"

Howbeit when he, the Spirit of truth, is come,
he will guide you into all truth: **for he shall not speak of himself; but whatsoever he shall hear, that shall he speak: and he will shew you things to come.**

John 16:13

The Spirit of God does not experience defeat, failure, or sin. He can only guide us into *all truth, victory, and success.* If we are led by the Spirit of God in all we do, ignorance will not be able to stand, because the Spirit of God will guide and lead us on the right pathway. We will stay on the right road. You see, we have no excuse to continue in sin.

Do not "try" not to sin. Simply make a decision not to sin. Then stick with your decision. When temptation comes, let the devil keep the temptation. How? Step apart from sin. Separate yourself unto a life of godliness.

Be ye not unequally yoked together with unbelievers: for what fellowship hath righteousness with unrighteousness? and what communion hath light with darkness?

And what concord hath Christ with Belial? or what part hath he that believeth with an infidel?

And what agreement hath the temple of God with idols? for ye are the temple of the living God; as God hath said, I will dwell in them, and walk in them; and I will be their God, and they shall be my people.

Wherefore come out from among them, and be ye separate, saith the Lord, and touch not the unclean thing; and I will receive you,

And will be a Father unto you, and ye shall be my sons and daughters, saith the Lord Almighty.

2 Corinthians 6:14-18

One of the most prominent corporate sins is gossip. Where corporate sin abounds, corporate judgment will come.

Corporate Sin

God's army is the only army I know of that kills its own wounded. In the medical field, doctors stand by doctors. Lawyers stand by lawyers. Family members stand by family members. Why cannot ministers stand by ministers?

King Saul made several attempts to kill David; yet, when Saul died, David wept bitterly. He said:

> **Tell it not in Gath, publish it not in the streets of Askelon; lest the daughters of the Philistines rejoice, lest the daughters of the uncircumcised triumph.**
>
> 2 Samuel 1:20

David was saying, "Don't tell the other lands our king is dead. Don't tell them how he died. Let's keep it quiet."

That is the way it should be in the Church. Don't publish the failures of other ministers and believers. Make sure your own life is right, then pray for that erring brother or sister. It is a sin not to stand by fellow believers and ministers and support them when they are going through a hard time.

As believers, we are to pour in the oil and the wine. We are to bind up the wounds. We are to keep the Church glorious. We are to sin no more. We are to live in holiness. We are to do what is right in the eyes of God.

We need to have a reverence toward the awesomeness of God — the mighty hand of God — knowing that from His breath He can bring destruction or blessing. Paul said:

Having therefore these promises, dearly beloved, let us cleanse ourselves from all filthiness of the flesh and spirit, perfecting holiness in the fear of God.

2 Corinthians 7:1

Only as we aim for perfection in holiness as a lifestyle, a way of life, will we hunger for spiritual things continually. Only as we step aside from sin and from things of the world will we want more of God.

. . . When he [Jesus] appears, we shall be like him, for we shall see him as he is.

Everyone who has this hope in him purifies himself, just as he is pure.

1 John 3:2,3 NIV

What a blessed assurance Jesus gave us in the Gospel of John as we make a decision to lay aside sin and the old flesh to hunger and thirst for more of Him.

. . . He who comes to Me will never be hungry and he who believes on and cleaves to and trusts in and relies on Me will never thirst any more — at any time.

John 6:35 AMP

Other Books by Roberts Liardon

I Saw Heaven

A Call To Action

The Invading Force

The Quest For Spiritual Hunger

The Price Of Spiritual Power

Religious Politics

Learning To Say No Without Feeling Guilty

Run to the Battle

Kathryn Kuhlman
A spiritual biography of God's miracle working power

Spiritual Timing

Breaking Controlling Powers

Cry of the Spirit
Unpublished sermons by Smith Wigglesworth

How To Survive An Attack

Haunted Houses Ghosts & Demons

Forget Not His Benefits

Holding To The Word Of The Lord

To contact Roberts Liardon
write:

Roberts Liardon Ministries
P.O. Box 30710, Laguna Hills, CA 92654

Please include your prayer requests and comments
when you write.

Additional copies of this book are available
from your local bookstore.

ALBURY PUBLISHING
P.O. Box 470406, Tulsa, OK 74137

Roberts Liardon Ministries International Offices:

In England, Europe, Eastern Europe, and Scandinavia

RLM EUROPE
PO BOX 295
WELWYN GARDEN CITY
HERTS, AL7 2QA, UK
TEL/FAX 44 1707 327222(UK)

In South Africa:

Embassy Christian Centre
PO Box 2233
Kimberley 8300
South Africa

Spirit Life Journal is Roberts Liardon's "pulpit to the world." Each colorful, bi-monthly issue will challenge, encourage and enlighten you with faith-building articles and Guest Pulpit articles from ministers around the world; plus special messages and features from Roberts.

For your free subscription, write:

ROBERTS LIARDON MINISTRIES
P.O. Box 30710
Laguna Hills, CA 92654

Be sure to print your complete address, zip code or country code.